CONTENTS

A BRIEF HISTORY OF
THE KYBALION

You have magical abilities that are inherent, inborn, and God-given. Since you were made in the image and likeness of the Creator, it makes sense that you have creative abilities and Divine power. One of your life's purposes is to learn how to harness your gifts into loving and positive action.

The Kybalion is a practical teaching manual for understanding and utilizing your Divinely magical abilities. First published in 1908, it's a classic esoteric self-help book that has taught countless people—including myself—how to put Hermetic (a term derived from Hermes, the name of the philosophy's originator) principles into action.

Because *The Kybalion*'s language is now dated and sometimes cryptic, I was guided to edit the manuscript into modern language and add my comments and practical application tools. Deeply honored by this assignment, I carefully and prayerfully edited *The Kybalion*, maintaining the integrity of its meanings and teachings. I only removed dated references, archaic phrasings, capitalizations, and redundancies from the authors' teachings. I left the original axioms from *The Kybalion* intact, out of respect for their ancient wisdom and tradition. My comments and examples are clearly distinguishable from the text of *The Kybalion* so you'll know what comes from me and what comes from the original authors.

About Hermetics

In ancient Egypt, a great spiritual teacher wrote books and lectured about the power of the mind to create and heal. His teachings were so profound and revolutionary that he was linked with Hermes, the Greek messenger deity; and Thoth, the Egyptian god of writing and mysticism. This teacher is most commonly called "Hermes Trismegistus" (pronounced: TRYS-mah-geest-us), which means "Thrice Great" or "Three Times Great." No one knows for certain which three attributes this title refers to.

While scholars can't agree on the dates of Hermes's life, it's believed that he was a contemporary (and even a teacher) of Abraham the Patriarch. Others claim that Hermes lived during the time of Moses. There's also controversy over the authenticity of

"The Emerald Tablet" or *Tabula Smaragdina* so often attributed to Hermes, which contains the famous "As above, so below" phrase.

Perhaps because of these controversies, Hermes's teachings have always been shrouded in veils of secrecy and mystery. Hermetic principles were only given to those who'd undergone initiations of purification, learning, and skill-building. The principles were primarily taught verbally and in secret.

Hermetic philosophy was incorporated into mystical Jewish teachings and the Alexandrian branch of Gnosticism (an ancient mystical Christian sect). Hermes's books, which include *The Corpus Hermeticum* and *The Divine Pymander,* were translated first into Greek, and then later into Arabic and Latin. Hermeticism and its offshoot, alchemy, were popular topics in the Middle Ages and Renaissance periods (roughly the years 800 through 1600). Among its fans were Sir Isaac Newton and Carl Jung.

During the Middle Ages, Hermetists studied in secret, since it was dangerous to write or verbalize any spiritual principle other than the reigning religions. To do so was to risk being killed as a "heretic" or "witch." The term "hermetically sealed" comes from this absolute secrecy surrounding Hermeticism.

Today, it's not only safe to study and practice Hermeticism, it's one of the healthiest ways to live. Most students of metaphysics understand that thoughts create reality. Yet, how do you control and focus your thoughts so that manifestations are at the highest and best level? I found the answer to that question within *The Kybalion*. It taught me a method that keeps my thoughts, and therefore my moods, health, relationships, finances, and such at a consistently high level.

The term *Kybalion* refers to the verbal teaching traditions of Hermetic principles, which were taught as axioms or phrases and then explained and expounded upon to initiates by advanced Hermetists. These individuals held the axioms in their memory banks and taught them to each other verbally. They weren't in any written form until 1908, when three Hermetists decided to publish them along with their interpretations.

The resulting book, *The Kybalion,* was authored by anonymous Hermetic teachers who called themselves "The Three Initiates" as a guide to the principles they'd learned through verbal traditions. Much speculation and controversy surrounds the identity of these three authors and the cryptic meaning of the term "Kybalion."

If you've read my books *Angel Medicine* or *Goddesses & Angels,* you know that I'm passionate about recovering the knowledge of ancient Egyptian, Mayan, and Greek teachings. The wisdom of these cultures (including Hermetics) have helped me better understand my past and present lives. *The Kybalion* is a wonderful distillation of these ancient teachings, and I believe you'll benefit from its messages.

The Kybalion requires some study. Read my comments and summaries first, and then read the writings of *The Kybalion* that follow. I believe that the best way to understand its teachings is by applying its principles to daily life. Read one principle and then hold the intention of looking for examples of its application in an everyday context. This can give you thunderbolt "Aha!" insights, which are the best learning tools.

The accompanying CD is a combination of my words and the original *Kybalion* teachings. It's an additional way to study the wisdom within this book.

It's been said that simply having *The Kybalion* nearby yields tremendous benefits, even if you don't read it. Its energy is pure magic, so you may want to keep this book on your nightstand to transfer its information into your unconscious while you sleep.

May you enjoy the further awakening of your power of Divine magic!

— **Doreen Virtue**

Author's Note: The italicized sentences within quotation marks are the original and unedited axioms from the verbal teaching traditions of Hermetic studies. These axioms are also indicated with a "— *The Kybalion*," just as in the book's original text. The other italicized words are the explanations of the axioms written by the Three Initiates. My comments and editorial remarks preceding each chapter of *The Kybalion* are in non-italicized type.

The following italicized and edited passages are from the introductory chapter of *The Kybalion*. In Chapters 2 through 12 and also the Afterword, my comments and summary precede each italicized *Kybalion* chapter.

INTRODUCTION TO
THE KYBALION

*"The lips of wisdom are closed, except
to the ears of Understanding"* — ***The Kybalion***

Old Egypt produced esoteric and occult teachings that have strongly influenced the philosophies of all races, nations, and peoples. Egypt, the home of the pyramids and the Sphinx, was the birthplace of hidden wisdom and mystical teachings.

The great adepts and masters dwelled in ancient Egypt. Among them was one hailed as "The Master of Masters." This man, if he was a mortal, lived during Egypt's earliest days. He was known as Hermes Trismegistus. He was the father of occult wisdom, the founder of astrology, and the discoverer of alchemy.

The details of his life story are lost to history, although several ancient countries disputed the details of his birthplace. The date of his sojourn in Egypt is not now known, but it has been fixed at the early days of the oldest dynasties of Egypt, long before the days of Moses. The best authorities regard him as a contemporary of Abraham. Some Jewish traditions claim that Abraham acquired a portion of his mystic knowledge from Hermes himself.

In all the ancient lands, the name of Hermes Trismegistus was revered, and his name became synonymous with the "Fount of Wisdom." We still use the term "hermetic" in the sense of "secret" or "sealed so that nothing can escape" because the followers of Hermes always observed secrecy in their teachings.

Hermetic teachings are found in all lands and among all religions. Yet they're never identified with any particular country or religious sect. The ancient teachers warned against allowing the Secret Doctrine to become crystallized into a creed. The wisdom of this caution is apparent to all students of history, which shows that when religion mixes with philosophy, the original occult wisdom is eventually lost.

Hermetics is not found in books. It has been passed verbally from master to student, from lip to ear. When it was written down at all, its meaning was veiled with terms of alchemy and astrology so that only those possessing the key could read it correctly. This was necessary to avoid the persecutions of theologians of the Middle

Ages, who fought the Secret Doctrine with fire, sword, stake, and cross. Even today, there are only a few reliable books on the Hermetic philosophy, although there are countless references to the topic in books on occultism. And yet, the Hermetic philosophy is the only master key that opens the doors of occult teachings!

In the early days, a compilation of basic Hermetic doctrines known as "The Kybalion" was passed verbally from teacher to student. The exact significance and meaning of the term <u>Kybalion</u> has been lost for several centuries. Its teachings have never been written down or printed, so far as we know. It was merely a collection of maxims and axioms that were incomprehensible to outsiders, but readily understood by students, after the axioms and maxims were explained by the Hermetic teachers.

These teachings were the basic principles of "The Art of Hermetic Alchemy," which dealt in the mastery of mental forces, rather than material elements of alchemically changing one kind of metal into another. The legend of the "Philosopher's Stone," which would turn base metal into gold, was a symbolic allegory relating to Hermetic philosophy.

In this little book, we invite our students to examine the Hermetic teachings within <u>The Kybalion</u> along with our explanations. We are humble students of the teachings, who are still students at the feet of Hermes, the Master. In this book, we give you many of the maxims, axioms, and precepts of <u>The Kybalion</u> accompanied by explanations that we feel will be most practical and comprehendible.

"Where fall the footsteps of the Master, the ears of those ready for his Teaching open wide. When the ears of the student are ready to hear, then cometh the lips to fill them with Wisdom."
— ***The Kybalion***

When the pupil is ready to receive the truth, then this little book will come to him or her. Such is The Law. The Hermetic principle of Cause and Effect, in its aspect of The Law of Attraction, will bring these teachings to whomever is prepared to receive them. So mote it be!

Chapter One

THE SEVEN SACRED SECRETS OF MANIFESTATION

Hermes's sacred teachings are divided into seven intercon-
nected principles in *The Kybalion*. The principles are nor-
mally studied in chronological order, as they build upon each
other.

Some of these principles may sound familiar, because spiritual teachers have been studying and writing about them since
Hermes introduced them centuries ago. So it may seem as if
you're studying basic arithmetic after you've already mastered
algebra.

Studying these principles builds a solid foundation for
your natural spiritual gifts. Although I'm a lifelong student and
practitioner of metaphysics, I discovered new wisdom, secrets,
and ideas by studying *The Kybalion*. A deeper understanding of
these principles helps you master your inborn manifestation

abilities. For instance, you'll learn how to maintain your moods, thoughts, and vibrations at high levels. This in turn keeps your relationships, finances, health, and other experiences at these same levels.

Here is an overview of the Seven Sacred Principles that Hermes gave us. The initial italicized sentences represent *The Kybalion*'s axiom as a synopsis of each principle. The chapters that follow give expanded information on each principle, as well as practical ways to put them into everyday use.

The Seven Sacred Principles

The First Sacred Principle is called *Mentalism. The Kybalion* axiom summarizing this principle is: *"The All is Mind; The Universe is Mental."*

This principle explains that the entire Universe (including yourself and your life) is composed of an all-encompassing Divine Mind, its thoughts, and thought forms.

The Kybalion refers to the Creator as "The All." The All is Mind, which means infinite and unerring intelligence, wisdom, and creativity. Since The All is everywhere, Mind is everywhere. You live inside this omnipresent Mind of The All.

Your true mind (your higher self) is an extension and a creation of the Divine Mind.

The Second Sacred Principle is called "Correspondence." *The Kybalion* summarizes this principle with Hermes's famous phrase: *"As above, so below; as below, so above."*

The Hermetists divide the world into three planes: physical, mental, and spiritual. Each plane operates by the same spiritual laws. So if you understand the laws governing one plane, you'll understand how the other planes operate. By applying this understanding, you can elevate your consciousness and life to higher planes of existence.

The Third Sacred Principle is called "Vibration." *The Kybalion* says: *"Nothing rests; everything moves; everything vibrates."*

Everything in the Universe moves, even so-called inanimate objects that are filled with vibrating atoms and the energy of The All. The difference between the varying planes of existence is merely in their vibrational rate of movement. Hermetists apply this principle by accelerating or decelerating the vibrational rate of objects or situations that they wish to attract, change, or banish.

The Fourth Sacred Principle is called "Polarity." *The Kybalion* summarizes it in this way: *"Everything is Dual; everything has poles; everything has its pair of opposites; like and unlike are the same; opposites are identical in nature, but different in degree; extremes meet; all truths are but half-truths; all paradoxes may be reconciled."*

The fourth principle explains that every experience and choice is the same in truth. What appears to be opposite is actually the same, but with different degrees of the same ingredients. Prosperity and poverty are not opposites. They are merely ends of the same pole, vibrating at different rates. Each situation in your life has such a pole, with extremes at either end and vibrational increments in between.

Hermetists use this principle to transmute unwanted situations and emotions into something more desirable, merely by changing their vibration to the highest end of each pole.

The Fifth Sacred Principle is called "Rhythm." *The Kybalion* axiom explaining this principle is: *"Everything flows, out and in; everything has its tides; all things rise and fall; the pendulum-swing manifests in everything; the measure of the swing to the right is the measure of the swing to the left; rhythm compensates."*

According to the fifth principle, the Universe operates in precise and predictable rhythms. If you allow these rhythms to master you, then your moods and life will fluctuate up and down. However, by mastering the rhythms, you become immune to downward turns in emotions or life experiences.

The Sixth Sacred Principle is called "Cause and Effect." *The Kybalion* says: *"Every Cause has its Effect; every Effect has its Cause; everything happens according to Law; Chance is but a name for Law not recognized; there are many planes of causation, but nothing escapes the Law."*

This is a perfectly ordered Universe, and nothing happens by chance or accident. There's always a Cause behind every Effect. Life mastery occurs when you become a conscious Cause of the Effects you desire, instead of being carried along by the wills or desires of others. You can use this principle to effect healings and manifestations.

The Seventh Sacred Principle is called "Gender." *The Kybalion*'s summary for this principle is: *"Gender is in everything; everything has its Masculine and Feminine Principles; Gender manifests on all planes."*

The seventh principle isn't referring to traditional male-female genders, as in human bodies. It instead discusses masculine and feminine energies. Each person has both energies within them, since the entire Universe is composed of both. These energies are equally powerful and interdependent upon each other to form creations.

Female energy is magnetic and attracting. Male energy is electric and creating. Banishing (releasing) and attracting are the basis of Divine magic. To manifest, you must either attract your desire or create it. To enjoy a steady flow of abundance, understand and work with the steady flow of giving and receiving, as this principle teaches.

"The Principles of Truth are Seven; he who knows these, understandingly, possesses the Magic Key before whose touch all the Doors of the Temple fly open."
— **The Kybalion**

Chapter Two

MENTAL ALCHEMY

No matter what's going on in your life that you'd like to banish or release, no matter what you'd like to attract or create . . . you can do so rapidly. One important aspect of Divine magic involves the process of transmutation.

Dictionaries define "transmutation" as:

1. A process of converting one element to another by irradiating or bombarding it with radioactive particles.

2. To change the form of, such as from kinetic to potential energy, or to modify the structure of a molecule, crystal, or atom.

3. Changing a gross force into a finer one.

4. The changing of energy into matter or matter into energy.

To the Hermetists, transmutation means to "change from an undesirable appearance into a desirable appearance." Note the word *appearance,* as it signifies that everything you want to attract or release is merely an illusion. It's a collection of energy, the same as thought. Therefore, it's just as easy to release or attract something major as it is to heal or manifest something less significant.

In the Middle Ages, the study of Hermetics and "alchemy" were considered underground crazes. Those who studied Hermetics were obsessed with turning base metals (such as lead) into precious metal (like gold). Yet Hermetists believe that "mental alchemy" is more valuable and important. Mental alchemy focuses upon attracting gold, and golden opportunities, through a process called "transmutation."

As *The Kybalion* discusses, you can transmute any object or situation by changing (or transmuting) your thoughts. Mental alchemy makes more sense as you study and practice the seven principles, as outlined in the chapters that follow.

"Mind (as well as metals and elements) may be transmuted, from state to state; degree to degree; condition to condition; pole to pole; vibration to vibration. True Hermetic Transmutation is a Mental Art." — **The Kybalion**

The Hermetists were the original alchemists, astrologers, and psychologists, and Hermes was the founder of these schools of thought. From astrology has grown modern astronomy; from alchemy has grown modern chemistry; from the mystic psychology has grown modern psychology.

There's much evidence that the ancients knew about and practiced astronomy, chemistry, and psychology. They possessed the inner knowledge as well as the outer knowledge, while scientists usually only have the outer knowledge. Transmutation was among the many secret branches of knowledge possessed by the Hermetists.

"Transmutation" usually refers to the ancient art of transmuting metals, particularly base metals, into gold. The word "transmute" means "to change from one nature, form, or substance, into another" (Webster's). And accordingly, "mental transmutation" means the art of changing and transforming mental states, forms, and conditions, into others. So we call mental transmutation the "Art of Mental Chemistry" or "Mental Alchemy."

The first of the Seven Hermetic Principles is the Principle of Mentalism. The axiom "The All is Mind; the Universe is Mental" *means that the underlying reality of the Universe is Mind and the Universe itself is Mental and "existing in the Mind of The All."*

If the Universe is mental in nature, then mental transmutation must be the art of changing the conditions of the Universe along the lines of matter, force, and mind. So mental transmutation is really the "magic" that ancient writers discussed in their mystical works, and about which they gave so few practical instructions. If everything is mental, then transmutation can not only change conditions ordinarily thought of as "mental," but also material conditions.

In this little book, we will outline the basic principles of mental transmutation, to help you better grasp the underlying principles and possess the master-key that unlocks the many doors of the Principle of Polarity.

In the next chapter, we'll discuss the first Hermetic Principle: the Principle of Mentalism, which explains the truth that "The All is Mind; the Universe is Mental," in the words of The Kybalion. We ask for your close attention and careful study of this great principle, for it's really the basic principle of the whole Hermetic philosophy, and of the Hermetic art of mental transmutation.

Chapter Three

SACRED PRINCIPLE NUMBER ONE: THE PRINCIPLE OF MENTALISM

The Universe and everything in it is continuously growing, moving, and changing. Nothing is permanent and enduring but change. The underlying power fueling this constant creation is called The All. It is all that is, and therefore infinite and eternal. The All is living mind consisting of an immortal life force and Divine wisdom. The All is Spirit.

The All occupies every space in the Universe. Spirit permeates your body, home, office, and automobile. There is no place where Spirit is not.

Unlike the Universe, which it powers and infinitely inhabits, The All is unchangeable. This paradox is reconciled through the Hermetic teaching that the Universe is contained within the Mind of The All. The container (The All) is unchangeable, but what's inside (The Universe) is forever changing.

In the same way, the contents of your mind are always changing. You can use this principle to change anything in your life. Since you create your own Universe with your mind (just like The All creates Universes with its Mind), you can alter its contents by changing your mind about your desires. Some processes for doing this are outlined in the chapters that follow.

First though, *The Kybalion* spends four chapters laying the foundation for its first principle, the Principle of Mentalism. It devotes only one chapter to each of the remaining six principles. That's because the first principle is so vital to understanding and applying the other principles and Hermetics in general. The concept of a mental Universe was a very radical concept when this book was first published. Even today, it's a new idea to those unfamiliar with metaphysics.

If you've already accepted the premise that everything in your life is thought forms, then you'll find this chapter and the three that follow to be quick reads. Nonetheless, I'd recommend staying present while reading each chapter, as there are some nuggets of wisdom that can help even the most seasoned metaphysician. These nuggets require careful study before they're apparent.

◇◇◇

*"Under, and back of, the Universe of Time, Space and Change, is ever to be found The Substantial Reality— the Fundamental Truth." — **The Kybalion***

Nothing really "is," but everything is "becoming" and changing. Nothing stands still because everything is being born, growing, and dying. The very instant a thing reaches its height, it begins to decline. The Principle of Rhythm is in constant operation. There is no reality or substantiality in anything. Nothing is permanent but change.

All things evolve from other things, and resolve into other things as a constant inflow and outflow, creation and destruction. All of these changing things are outward appearances or manifestations of an underlying power that Hermetic masters call "The All." The inner nature of The All is unknowable. Only The All can comprehend its own nature and being.

But while the essential nature of The All is unknowable, there are certain truths connected with its existence that The Kybalion teaches: "That which is the Fundamental Truth, the Substantial Reality, is beyond true naming, but wise men call it The All. In its essence, The All is unknowable. But, the report of reason must be hospitably received, and treated with respect." Human reason makes the following conclusions regarding The All, without attempting to remove the veil of the unknowable:

(1) The All must be All there really is. Nothing could exist outside of The All, or else The All would not be The All.

(2) The All must be infinite, for nothing could define, confine, bound, limit, or restrict The All. It must be infinite in time, or eternal. The All must have always and continuously existed, for there is nothing else that could have created it. Something cannot evolve from nothing. If The All had ever "not been," even for a moment, it would not "be" now. It must continuously exist forever, since nothing can destroy it.

The All must be infinite in space everywhere, because there is no place outside of The All. It must be continuous in Space, without break, cessation, separation, or interruption, since nothing could break, separate, or interrupt its continuity. It must be infinite in power, or absolute, because nothing could limit, restrict, restrain, confine, disturb, or condition it. It is subject to no other Power, because there is no other Power.

(3) The All must be immutable and unchangeable, since there is no force outside of it to effect changes. It cannot be added to nor subtracted from, increased nor diminished, nor become greater or lesser. It must have always been, and must always remain, just what it is now: The All.

Since the All is infinite, absolute, eternal, and unchangeable, by logical deduction we can reason that anything that is changeable cannot be The All. And since there is nothing outside of The All, then any and all such finite things must be nothing in reality. We will reconcile this apparent contradiction very soon.

The All is not matter or mere energy, since nothing can rise higher than its source. What is higher than matter or energy that we know to exist in the Universe? Life and Mind in their varying degrees of unfoldment! The All is "Infinite Living Mind," a term far higher than mechanical forces, or matter. The All is the Infinite Living Mind, which we call "Spirit!"

Chapter Four

THE MENTAL
UNIVERSE

*T*he *Kybalion* thoroughly examines the nature of the Universe using Hermes's "As above, so below" deductive reasoning. Hermetics teaches that if you understand one plane of existence, you can understand all other planes. So the Hermetists' conclusions about the Universe and The All come from applying earthly knowledge to these higher planes. They conclude that the "above" (the Universe) expands and creates just like the "below" (matter) through mental images.

You create your own Universe with the mental images that you hold, a principle that *The Kybalion* has much to say and teach about in the following chapters. This chapter continues to set the foundation for the first Hermetic principle of Mentalism. It's necessary to understand this principle before the other ones make sense.

"The Universe is Mental—held in the Mind of The All."
— ***The Kybalion***

The All is Spirit! But what is Spirit? This question cannot be answered, because Spirit is The All, which cannot be explained or defined. Spirit is simply a name given to the highest conception of Infinite Living Mind. Spirit transcends our understanding, and we use the term as a way to think or speak of The All, while simultaneously acknowledging that we cannot fully understand it. We must either do this or stop thinking of the matter at all.

Let's now consider the nature of the Universe, as a whole and in its parts. What is the Universe? We have seen that there can be nothing outside of The All. Then is the Universe The All? No, this cannot be, because the Universe is constantly changing, and in other ways does not measure up to The All, as stated in our last lesson.

At first, the human mind might deduce that if the Universe isn't The All, it must be nothing. But this is not a satisfying answer, since we are aware of the Universe's existence. Then if the Universe is neither The All, nor nothing, what can it be? Let us examine this question.

If the Universe exists at all, or seems to exist, it must be The All's creation. But as something can never come from nothing, what substance did The All use to create the Universe? Some philosophers believe The All created the Universe from itself. But The All cannot subtract or divide itself to become an atom or earthly being. Other philosophers have jumped to the conclusion that they and The All are identical. They shout, "I Am God!" This is similar to a vein declaring that it is the entire human body.

But what is the Universe, if it's not The All separated into fragments? What else can it be, and what can it be made of? The second principle, the "Principle of Correspondence" and the old Hermetic axiom, "As above, so below" help us glimpse the workings on higher planes by examining those on our own.

On the material earthly plane, humans create by using outside materials. But this analogy doesn't answer our question since there are no materials outside of The All to be used in creating the Universe. Humans also procreate their children with a portion of their own selves. But this scenario is also counter to our knowledge that The All can't transfer or subtract a portion of itself. Nor can anything add to or multiply The All.

So is there a third way that humans create? Yes, they create mentally! Mental creations use no outside materials, and don't involve reproducing or fragmenting oneself. And yet, each human's Spirit pervades their mental creations.

Following the Principle of Correspondence ("As above, so below"), we can deduce that The All creates the Universe mentally, in the same manner humans create mental images. Such was the teaching of Hermes: The All can create in no other way except mentally, without either using material (and there is nothing outside of itself to use), or else reproducing itself (since one times one equals one).

Just as you may create a Universe of your own in your mind, so does The All create Universes in its own Mentality. Your Universe is the mental creation of a finite mind, whereas that of The All is the creation of an Infinite. The two are similar, but infinitely different in degree. We shall examine more closely the process of creation and manifestation as we proceed. But this is the point to fix in your minds at this stage: The Universe and all it contains is a mental creation of The All.

> *"The All creates in its Infinite Mind countless Universes, which exist for eons of Time—and yet, to The All, the creation, development, decline and death of a million Universes is as the time of the twinkling of an eye."*
> *— The Kybalion*

> *"The Infinite Mind of The All is the womb of Universes."*
> *— The Kybalion*

The All and the Principle of Gender

The seventh Hermetic principle, the Principle of Gender (which states that everything in the Universe is composed of male and female energies) is manifested on all planes of life, material, mental, and spiritual. Whenever anything is generated or created on any plane of existence, the Principle of Gender must be involved. This is true even in the creation of Universes.

The All itself is beyond Gender, as it is beyond every other Law, including those of Time and Space. The All is the Law from which all Laws proceed, and it is not subject to them. But when The All manifests on the lower planes, then it acts according to Law and Principle. Consequently, it manifests the Principle of Gender, in its Masculine and Feminine aspects, on the Mental Plane.

The All itself does not have duality and therefore gender. The All is One and the masculine and feminine principles are manifested by The All. The masculine principle is manifested when The All projects its will toward the feminine principle (which may be called "Nature"). Nature then begins the actual work of evolving the Universe, including humans and the higher planes.

If you prefer the old figures of thought, you may think of the masculine principle as God the Father, and the feminine principle as Nature, the Universal Mother from whose womb all things have been born. This isn't just a poetic figure of speech. It describes the actual process of the Universe's creation. The All is One, and the Universe (including the masculine and feminine principles) is generated, created, and exists within its Infinite Mind.

It may be helpful in your understanding to apply the Principle of Correspondence to yourself and your own mind. The part of You which you call "I" stands apart and witnesses the creation of mental images in your own mind. The part of your mind that creates mental images may be called the "Me" in contrast to the "I," which stands apart and witnesses and examines the thoughts, ideas, and images of the "Me." The "I" is your inner Masculine Principle, and your "Me" is your Feminine Principle. Each person carries both genders within themselves.

Like a child, we naturally feel reverence for The All, as it is our Father and Mother Mind. The feelings you have of love and nurturing from religion, spirituality, and nature are like a child's affection for its parents.

The earth is one small aspect of the Universe, which also includes millions of other worlds. There are also millions of other Universes in existence within the Infinite Mind. There are beings with powers and attributes higher than humans have ever dreamed of. And yet these beings were once as you, or even on lower planes. They will continue to grow even higher, in time, for this is the destiny of all souls.

Death is not real, even in the relative sense. It is merely birth into a new life. You shall go on to higher planes of life, for eons of time. The Universe is your home, and you shall explore its farthest recesses before the end of time. You are dwelling in the Infinite Mind of The All, and your possibilities and opportunities are infinite, both in time and space. And at the end of the Grand Cycle of Eons, when The All draws all of its creations back into itself, you will go gladly because by so doing, you will truly experience oneness with The All.

And, in the meantime, rest calm and serene. You are safe and protected by the infinite power of the Father-Mother Mind.

"Within the Father-Mother Mind, mortal children are at home. There is not one who is Fatherless nor Motherless in the Universe."
— The Kybalion

Chapter Five

THE DIVINE PARADOX

This chapter discusses the paradox that matter is illusory *and* real, simultaneously. The trick is to enjoy the material world without losing yourself in its illusions.

The Kybalion says the Divine Paradox is "that while the Universe is not, still it is." There's a difference between Absolute Truth and Relative Truth. Only the Creator knows the Absolute Truth of the Universe.

Relative Truth is the human understanding that matter exists because we can touch, smell, see, hear, and taste it. Relative Truth is based upon our human experiences, without the whole knowledge of Absolute Truth behind it. We experience material objects as being solid. However, electronic microscopes show that seemingly solid objects are really composed of vibrating atoms, which are contained within and fueled by The All.

Hermetics teaches that it's a mistake to go through life as if everything is an illusion. They call this practice "sleepwalking through life." Ignoring or denying matter doesn't help us live effectively. While we live in human bodies on Earth, it's important to acknowledge that matter is real to us. And yet, we can change our relationship with matter by elevating our thoughts about it. This is how we practice Divine magic to heal bodies, attract prosperity, and complete important projects.

We can gain control over our material existence first by acknowledging matter's existence within the illusion, and then by applying the higher forces of transmutation and Mental Creation (a process that *The Kybalion* explains throughout the text).

∞◇∞

"The half-wise, recognizing the comparative unreality of the Universe, imagine that they may defy its laws. Such are vain and presumptuous fools, and they are broken against the rocks and torn asunder by the elements by reason of their folly. The truly wise, knowing the nature of the Universe, use Law against laws; the higher against the lower; and by the Art of Alchemy transmute that which is undesirable into that which is worthy, and thus triumph. Mastery consists not in abnormal dreams, visions and fantastic imaginings or living, but in using the higher forces against the lower—escaping the pains of the lower planes by vibrating on the higher. Transmutation, not presumptuous denial, is the weapon of the Master." — **The Kybalion**

The above axiom describes the paradox of the Universe, resulting from the Principle of Polarity that manifests when The All begins to create. The Infinite All sees the Universe and everything within it as a dream within a state of meditation. Yet, to our finite awareness, the Universe must be treated as real, and lived with an understanding of the higher truth.

If humans act and live as if the Universe is only a dream, then they're like sleep-walkers stumbling through life and making no progress. They're forced awake when the natural laws, which they try to ignore, bruise them. Keep your mind ever on the star, but let your eyes watch over your footsteps, to avoid falling should your focus be too far upward. The fact is that you are on Earth now, and you must deal with its nature and laws. You can, however, enjoy your life if you work with the mental laws, which are higher than the material laws.

What Hermetists know as "The Law of Paradox" is an aspect of the Principle of Polarity. Hermetic writings are filled with references to paradoxes in life. Hermetic teachers constantly encourage their students to consider the "other side" of any question. We encourage you to study and grasp the Divine Paradox of the Absolute and Relative, to avoid entanglement in the mire of the half-truth.

You may instinctually protest the idea that the Universe is a mental creation of The All, and therefore an illusion. So, consider both the Absolute and Relative points of view.

Absolute Truth is defined as "Things as the mind of God knows them." The Absolute Truth is that the forever-changing Universe is an illusion when it's compared to the forever unchangeable All. Anything that has a beginning and an ending must be, in a sense, unreal and untrue, and the Universe comes under this category. From the Absolute point of view, there is nothing real except The All.

Now let's consider Relative Truth, which is defined as "things as the highest reasoning of humans can understand." So while the Universe is unreal and illusionary, to the finite minds viewing it through mortal senses, the Universe is very real. We must consider the experience of the human senses, because we are humans. We are not The All.

If you kick a rock, for example, it doesn't matter that science has proven that the rock isn't solid. Your foot feels the impact with the rock. Of course, your foot is matter just like the rock and brain. If you were to dream about the rock, your mental image of it would seem very real. Because we live within the illusionary Universe, it seems very real to us. To know it otherwise, we must be The All itself. Only when The All finally withdraws us into itself will the illusion actually vanish.

So there's no point in dwelling upon the topic of illusion. Instead, let's direct our attention to the real nature of the Universe. Let's aspire to understand its mental laws and use them to progress through life. The mental laws are ironclad within the Universe's mental nature. Everyone except for The All is bound by them.

As long as we live on the material Earth plane, matter is real to us. Matter isn't less real to us just because we understand the scientific truth about atoms, or the Hermetic teachings about the mental nature of the Universe.

We can control matter by applying higher forces. This is better than pretending that matter doesn't exist. The laws of nature are constant and we can't escape them. We can, however, overcome the laws by applying higher ones.

The Universe and its laws and phenomena are real, so far as humans are concerned. The Universe is also ever-changing and transitory, so it's unreal in the Absolute sense. However, we must live and act as if the fleeting Universe and matter were real. In the material world, Mentalism, the power of your thought, is the greatest natural force.

Remember <u>The Kybalion</u>'s wise words: "Mastery consists not in abnormal dreams, visions and fantastic imaginings or living, but in using the higher forces against the lower—escaping the pains of the lower planes by vibrating on the higher." Remember always, student, that "transmutation, not presumptuous denial, is the weapon of the Master."

We do not live in a world of dreams, but in a Universe which is real as far as our lives and actions are concerned. Our business in the Universe is not to deny its existence, but to live, using the Laws to rise from lower to higher and doing the best that we can under the circumstances arising each day.

There's nothing to fear, as we're all held firmly in the Infinite Mind of The All. There is no power outside of the All to affect us, so we can rest calm and secure.

Chapter Six

"THE ALL" IN ALL

After examining the paradoxical Universe, *The Kybalion* next studies the Creator using the same Hermetic "As above, so below" deductive reasoning.

When an author creates a character (such as Shakespeare's Romeo), part of the author is in the character. In the same way, part of the Creator is in each of us. Yet, just as Romeo isn't entirely Shakespeare, neither are we entirely the Creator.

We retain some part of us that's not identical with our Creator—this is another Divine Paradox. We're simultaneously made in the image, and not in the image, of the Creator. We would call the part of us that isn't Creator-like the "ego" or our "shadow side."

"While All is in The All, it is equally true that The All is in All. To him who truly understands this truth hath come great knowledge."
— **The Kybalion**

We have given you the Hermetic teaching regarding the mental nature of the Universe, the truth that "the Universe is Mental—held in the Mind of The All."

Now let's examine the above quote from <u>The Kybalion</u>: "All is in The All. It is equally true that The All is in All." This apparently contradictory statement is reconcilable under the Law of Paradox. Even more, it's an exact Hermetic statement of the relationship between The All and its mental Universe.

The All is omnipresent throughout every particle of the Universe. It's much like a character in a novel. While reading the novel, the character seems to have a life force of its own. Yet the character also carries the essence of the author. In fact the character's entire life and reality comes from the mental images of the author.

The characters Othello and Hamlet existed merely in the mind of Shakespeare at the time of their conception and creation. And yet Shakespeare also existed within each of these characters, giving them their vitality, spirit, and action. Whose is the "spirit" of these characters. Is it Shakespeare, or do these characters have a personal spirit, independent of their creator? Do they have reality on their own, or do they represent the spiritual and mental power of their author?

The Law of Paradox says that both propositions are true. Hamlet is both Hamlet and also Shakespeare. And yet Shakespeare is not identical with Hamlet. Hamlet may exclaim: "The spirit of my Creator is within me and yet I am not He!" This truth gives sharp contrast to the often-heard cries of "I am God!" which would be identical to Hamlet shouting: "I am Shakespeare!"

The All is in the earthworm, yet the earthworm is far from being The All. And though the earthworm appears as a lowly being, it was created within the Mind of The All. So, The All is immanent in the earthworm and all the particles of its makeup.

Even these illustrations are inadequate, since they are creations of our finite minds, while the Universe is a creation of Infinite Mind. The difference between the two poles separates them, yet it is merely a matter of degree as the Principle of Correspondence reminds us: "As above, so below; as below, so above."

To the degree that you realize the existence of Spirit within your being, so will you rise in the spiritual scale of life. This is what spiritual development means. There are many planes of existence in the Universe, with the lowest being dense matter and the upper being the Spirit of The All. Everything is moving upward along this scale of life. All progress is a return to Home.

The All creates by projecting its Will with the intention of "Becoming." This projection of The All's Will then slows its vibration so that matter is created. This process is called "Involution," in which The All becomes involved or wrapped-up with its creation. This is analogous to artists who forget their own existence while creating. The artists temporarily live within and through their creations, and therefore transfer their life force to their artwork.

As you'll read in the chapter about the Principle of Polarity, everything in the Universe has a pole with two extremes of low and high energy at either end, and degrees of energy in-between. The Involuntionary stage of creation is sometimes called the "outpouring of Divine energy." The extreme pole of the Creative process is the furthest from The All. The other extreme called the Evolutionary Stage (also known as "Indrawing") is the idea of coming home.

This Involutionary stage of Creation is sometimes called the "Outpouring" of Divine Energy, just as the Evolutionary state is called the "Indrawing" of Divine energy. The Involutionary stage is the extreme pole of the Creative process. It's considered to the furthest removed from The All, while the beginning of the Evolutionary stage is the closest.

As you'll read in the chapter about the Principle of Rhythm, everything in the Universe swings pendulum-like along the poles described in the Principle of Polarity. During The All's outpouring of Divine energy, the vibrations become subsequently lower until finally the momentum ceases. This is the beginning of the return pendulum swing to the Evolutionary end of the creative pole.

During the Outpouring stage, The All's creative forces manifest as a compact whole. Then during the Evolutionary or Indrawing stage, the creations become individualized. As the pendulum swings upward toward the highest vibrations of The All upon the pole of creation, the individuals return to their Source.

The ancient Hermetists used the word "meditation" to describe the process of the mental creation of the Universe in the Mind of The All. They also used the phrase "Divine Attention" to describe The All's creative process, as the word "attention" comes from a Latin word meaning "reaching out or extending." So, Divine Attention means an extension of The All's mental energy.

The Hermetists use the term "evolution" to refer to the ascension or spiritual growth process. Evolution occurred first when The All meditated upon the beginning of the Creation and established the material foundations of the Universe by thinking it into existence. After this, The All gradually awakened from its meditation. Like a sleeping man slowly moving from a reclining to a standing position, the Universe responded to The All's awakening by moving to higher energy vibrations. Eventually, the spirit of each soul is infinitely expanded, and the Creator and the Created are merged.

Creation and Evolution takes eons of earthly time, with each eon consisting of millions of years. Yet the Universe's entire cycle of Involution and Evolution happened in the blink of an eye from The All's perspective.

This illustration of the "meditation," and subsequent "awakening from meditation" of The All is only an attempt of the teachers to describe the Infinite process by a finite example. And yet: "As Below, so Above." The difference is merely in degree. And just as The All arouses itself from the meditation upon the Universe, so do humans cease from manifesting upon the material plane, and withdraw themselves more into their indwelling Spirit.

You may wonder why The All creates Universes? This question has been asked and pondered for ages. Some have imagined that The All had something to gain by it, but this is absurd, for what could The All gain that it did not already possess? Others have proposed that The All wished something to love. Some believe that it created for pleasure or amusement, because it was lonely, or to manifest its power.

Another theory is that The All was compelled to create, by reason of its own internal nature and creative instinct. Yet, the idea of The All being compelled implies a force outside of itself, which is impossible. The theory also implies that the creative instinct would be the Absolute, instead of The All, which is also impossible. Yet, The All does create and manifest. The All's nature also seems to correspond to humanity's creative instincts, according to the Principle of Correspondence.

The All could not act unless it willed to act, and it would not will to act unless it desired to act, and it would not desire to act unless it obtained some satisfaction from it. We still prefer to think that The All acted entirely free of any external or internal influences.

There cannot be a reason for The All to act, for a reason implies that there's a cause. The All is above the Principle of Cause and Effect, which is a law of the Universe and not of The All. The only exception is when The All wills to become a Cause, which sets the principle into motion.

Since The All is unknowable, we are content to say that The All simply "is." From this, we conclude that The All acts because it acts. The All is complete reason in itself, and also all law and action in itself. In other words, The All is its own reason, law, and action. Even further, The All is one with reason, law, and action.

We believe that the answer to the question, "Why does The All create Universes?" is locked up in the inner self of The All, along with its secret of being. The Principle of Correspondence reaches only to The All's aspect of "becoming." Behind that is The All's nature of being, in which all principles and laws are merged into oneness. Therefore, metaphysical speculation on this point is futile. We recognize the question; however, ordinary answers fade under logical examinations.

Legend says that when Hermes was asked this same question by advanced students, he answered them by pressing his lips tightly together without uttering a word. This indicated there was no answer. He may have also been conveying the Hermetic axiom:

"The lips of Wisdom are closed, except to the ears of Understanding," believing that even his advanced students did not possess the necessary understanding. At any rate, if Hermes possessed the secret, he didn't impart it. As far as the world is concerned, the lips of Hermes are still closed on this point. And if Hermes hesitated to answer the question, why would we suppose anyone else would know the answer?

If the question is at all answerable, the Hermetic truth applies: *"While All is in The All, it is equally true that The All is in All. To him who truly understands this truth, hath come great knowledge."*

Chapter Seven

SACRED PRINCIPLE
NUMBER TWO:
THE PRINCIPLE OF
CORRESPONDENCE

After laying the foundation with a thorough examination of the nature of the mental Universe and The All, *The Kybalion* now picks up speed. Up to this point, *The Kybalion* has presented fascinating philosophical discussion, without giving much practical advice or application.

With this and subsequent chapters (especially the fourth Principle of Polarity), you'll learn some ways to apply Hermetic knowledge to improve your daily life.

The Principle of Correspondence refers to the three levels (or planes) of existence: physical, mental, and spiritual. Each plane vibrates at different rates, and these vibrational differences are the only distinguishing factors between planes. Otherwise, all three planes are aspects of The All. The higher spiritual planes vibrate the fastest, and the lower material planes vibrate the slowest (which is why matter appears dense and solid).

The material plane is divided into subcategories of matter, ethereal substance, and energy, with the latter having the fastest vibrations. Similarly, the mental plane is subdivided into (from lower to higher vibrations) the mineral, plant, elemental, animal, and human mind. The mineral mind is the thought force within the mineral kingdom, the plant mind is the intelligence within plants, and so forth. The spiritual plane also has its subcategories of angels, archangels, and deities.

"As above, so below" also applies to the three planes and their subcategories. *The Kybalion* says: "There is a correspondence, harmony, and agreement between the several planes." The Principle of Correspondence, as well as the remaining Principles of Vibration, Polarity, Rhythm, Cause and Effect, and Gender, manifest and operate upon each plane.

◇◆◇

"As above, so below; as below, so above." — ***The Kybalion***

The second Hermetic principle describes the harmony, agreement, and correspondence between the planes of manifestation, life, and being. Everything in the Universe comes from the same source. So, regardless of which plane something exists upon, it's subject to the same laws, principles, and characteristics as everything else.

Hermetic philosophy holds that the Universe is divided into three great classes of phenomena, known as the Three Great Planes:

I.   The Great Physical Plane
II. The Great Mental Plane
III. The Great Spiritual Plane

These divisions are artificial and arbitrary, because the three planes are ascending degrees of the scale of life, from the lowest point of matter to the highest point of Spirit. The different planes shade into each other, without hard distinctions between the higher phenomena of the physical and the lower of the mental, for example. In short, the Three Great Planes are groupings of degrees of life manifestation.

The planes are neither places nor dimensions of space. Yet, they are more than states or conditions. The planes don't have the ordinary dimensions of length, depth, and breadth, but they do have a "fourth dimension" of vibration.

The Universe is in constant motion at different vibrational rhythms, speeds, rates, and directions. So, the only variable separating one plane from another is its vibration. The higher the vibrational rate, the higher the plane. Other than the vibrational differences, all of the planes are fundamentally the same as creations of The All existing within the Infinite Mind.

Each of the Three Great Planes are subdivided into seven minor planes, which are also subdivided into seven sub-planes. All these divisions are arbitrary, since they blend into each other. The divisions are mostly for convenience of study and thought.

The Physical Plane

The Great Physical Plane and its seven minor planes includes everything physical and material, along with physics, energy, forces, and manifestations. Keep in mind that Hermetics views matter as a dense form of energy with slow vibrations. So Heremetists classify matter under the category of "energy," and assign it three of the seven minor planes of the Great Physical Plane.

These Seven Minor Physical Planes are as follows:

I. The Plane of Matter (A)
II. The Plane of Matter (B)

III. *The Plane of Matter (C)*
IV. *The Plane of Ethereal Substance*
V. *The Plane of Energy (A)*
VI. *The Plane of Energy (B)*
VII. *The Plane of Energy (C)*

The Plane of Matter (A) includes matter in solids, liquids, and gases. The Plane of Matter (B) comprises higher, subtler, and radiant forms of matter such as radioactive waves and particles. The Plane of Matter (C) involves the most subtle and tenuous Matter, the existence of which is not suspected by ordinary scientists. The Plane of Ethereal Substance is composed of ether, an extremely elastic substance that pervades all universal space, and which is the medium for energy waves.

Next highest in vibrational frequency is the Plane of Energy (A), which includes heat, light, magnetism, electricity, and attraction (such as gravity, cohesion, and chemical affinity). The Plane of Energy (B) comprises higher forms of energy not yet discovered by science. Known as "Nature's Finer Forces," they conduct the energy of mental phenomena such as telepathy. The Plane of Energy (C) includes energy so highly organized that it bears many of the characteristics of "life." This energy is only known to beings of the Spiritual Plane and to those who know and experience this plane while still living upon the earth.

The Mental Plane

The Great Mental Plane includes living things known to us in ordinary life, as well as other forms known only to occultists. As with the material plane, the Mental Plane is subdivided into seven minor planes which are:

I. The Plane of Mineral Mind.
II. The Plane of Elemental Mind (A).
III. The Plane of Plant Mind.
IV. The Plane of Elemental Mind (B).
V. The Plane of Animal Mind.
VI. The Plane of Elemental Mind (C).
VII. The Plane of Human Mind.

The Plane of Mineral Mind comprises the conditions of the entities that animate the minerals and chemicals. These entities are not to be confused with molecules and atoms, which are merely the material forms of these entities, just as a man's body is his material form and not "himself."

These entities may be called "souls," who are living beings of slow vibration at a rate slightly faster than the living energy of the highest Physical Plane. The average person usually doesn't recognize the mind, soul, or life within the mineral kingdom. However, *all occultists recognize this existence, and modern science is rapidly moving toward the point of view of the Hermetic, in this respect.*

Molecules, atoms, and corpuscles have their likes and dislikes, and attractions and repulsions. Some of the more daring scientists have postulated that the emotions and feelings of atoms differ only in degree from those of men. All occultists know this to be a fact.

The Plane of Elemental Mind (A) includes the most basic elemental beings. Although they are invisible to the ordinary senses of humans, they exist and play their part of the drama of the Universe. Their degree of intelligence is between that of the mineral and chemical entities on the one hand, and of the entities of the plant kingdom on the other.

The Plane of Plant Mind is composed of the kingdoms of the Plant World. Plants have life, mind, and soul. The Plane of Elemental Mind (B), involves higher vibrating and more intelligent elementals than the (A) Elemental Plane. The Plane of Animal Mind comprises the entities, beings, or souls animating the animal forms of life. The Plane of Elemental Mind (C), are the highest vibrational and most intelligent elemental beings, such as fairies, elves, leprechauns, and such.

The Plane of Human Mind is the human life and mentality. This plane, like the others, has seven sub-categories from the slowest vibrational rate of low intelligence, to the highest rate of spiritual wisdom and intelligence. It has taken the human race millions of years to collectively reach the fourth subdivision of vibration and intelligence. Some advanced souls are vibrating at the level of the fifth, sixth, or seventh subdivisions. Some humans even exist on the lower levels of the next highest plane, the Great Spiritual Plane.

The Spiritual Plane

The Great Spiritual Plane, like the other planes, has seven subdivisions called minor planes, which also have seven subdivisions of their own. This plane encompasses beings whose life, mind, and form vibrate at the highest rates. Humans who have reached the level of adept or avatar are at the lowest subdivision of this plane. Above them are the angels, archangels, ascended masters, and deities. These unseen divinities and angelic helpers extend their influence freely and powerfully in the process of evolution and cosmic progress. They also intervene and assist in human affairs.

Yet even the highest of these advanced beings is still a creation existing in the Mind of The All, and still subject to universal laws. In that sense, they are still mortal because they belong to the Universe and are subject to its conditions.

According to the Principle of Correspondence, which embodies the truth: "As above, so below; as below, so above," all of the Seven Hermetic Principles are in full operation on every plane of existence. There is a correspondence, harmony, and agreement between the planes.

"As above, so below; as below, so above." This centuries-old Hermetic axiom embodies one of the great principles of universal phenomena. As we consider the remaining Principles, we will clearly see the truth within the Principle of Correspondence.

Chapter Eight

SACRED PRINCIPLE NUMBER THREE: THE PRINCIPLE OF VIBRATION

Hermes taught that everything constantly moves and never rests long before microscopes proved the validity of his postulation. Vibration is what distinguishes and differentiates the planes of correspondence discussed in the previous chapter.

The All vibrates at a constant and steady high rate. The slowest vibratory rates are found in matter. The other planes of correspondence vibrate at rates in between these two extremes.

The material plane is composed of vibrating atoms. If a material object was spun around (or vibrated) fast enough, the human senses could no longer see or hear the object. The object would leave the material plane and move upward in frequency to the mental and spiritual planes. Similarly, you can raise the vibrations of objects and thoughts to move them to higher planes of existence.

Each thought, emotion, or mental state vibrates at different frequencies, much like musical notes. Just as you can deliberately play a specific musical note, so can you choose to deliberately hold specifically high vibrating thoughts, emotions, and mental states.

Every thought, emotion, and desire vibrates and attracts experiences of matching vibrations. If you'd like to attract better experiences, you must elevate your thoughts and emotions. The Principle of Vibration explains that you can polarize your mind at any vibrational degree you wish, and so gain perfect control over your mental states, moods, and experiences.

A portion of your thought vibrations affects the minds of other people, a phenomenon called "induction" or "telepathy." You can deliberately uplift the vibrations of those around you by elevating and radiating your positive thoughts. You can also change the vibrations of material objects to attract them into your life, to fix broken items, or release anything that's unwanted.

Those who study and practice the Principle of Vibration are using a higher law than "physical laws," thereby seeming to defy gravity, time, and space to accomplish miracles. *The*

Kybalion says: "He who understands the Principle of Vibration has grasped the sceptre of Power."

◇◇◇

"Nothing rests; everything moves; everything vibrates."
— **The Kybalion**

The third Hermetic principle—the Principle of Vibration—embodies the truth that motion is manifest in everything in the Universe. Nothing is at rest; everything moves, vibrates, and circles.

This Hermetic principle was recognized by early Greek philosophers who embodied it in their systems. But, then, for centuries the principle was forgotten. It was rediscovered in the nineteenth century when scientists unlocked the secrets of atoms and radioactivity. Science now realizes that matter and energy are modes of vibratory motion, and soon science will discover the same within mental phenomena.

The differences between the various manifestations within the Universe are due entirely to varying vibrational rates. Even The All manifests a constant and intensely rapid vibration. Spirit is at one end of the Pole of Vibration, and the other pole is extremely dense and slow-vibrating forms of matter. Between these two poles are millions of different rates and modes of vibration.

◇◇◇

Daily life provides concrete examples of the effects of increased vibrations. As musical notes get higher in pitch, their vibrational rate increases. Eventually, the notes and vibrations are so high that they are imperceptible. Colors are another example. Red is the lowest vibrational color the human eye can see, and violet is at the top of the spectrum. There are even higher notes, colors, and energies that are beyond human perception.

When an object vibrates fast enough, its molecules disintegrate and resolve themselves into the original atoms. Then the atoms, following the Principle of Vibration, are separated into the countless electrons and protons of which they are composed. With a high enough frequency of vibration, even these elements will eventually scatter. The remaining essence of the object is then composed of ethereal substance. The faster vibrations liberate the object's light, heat, and other energy from its previously confining molecules and atoms. If the vibrations were further increased, the dematerialized object would climb the successive mental and spiritual planes, until it would finally reenter The All.

Just as a musical note may be reproduced by causing an instrument to vibrate at a certain rate, so can mental states be reproduced at will. In other words, you can control your mental state, and lift your vibrations to any level you choose.

Every thought, emotion, reason, will, desire, or mental state, is accompanied by vibrations, a portion of which affects the minds of other people through "induction." This produces telepathy and other forms of psychic phenomena and mental influence.

With a little reflection, you'll see that the Principle of Vibration underlies the wonderful phenomena and power manifested by masters and adepts who set aside natural laws. In reality, they are simply using one law against another to accomplish their results. They have learned to change the vibrations of material objects and other forms of energy and perform "miracles." Remember the Hermetic axiom: "He who understands the Principle of Vibration has grasped the sceptre of Power."

Chapter Nine

SACRED PRINCIPLE NUMBER FOUR: THE PRINCIPLE OF POLARITY

The Principle of Polarity could also be called "The Principle of Practicality," since it offers a profoundly practical tool for living, manifesting, healing, and practicing Divine magic. The first three principles have discussed how the material, mental, and spiritual planes are from the same energy which the Hermetists call The All. The differences in planes are purely because they vibrate at differing rates.

The Fourth Principle states that everything has two polarities or extremes. These seeming opposites are part of the same pole, and they're just situated at different ends. For example, hot and cold are extremes of the pole called "temperature."

The Kybalion says: "The difference between things diametrically opposed to each other is merely a matter of degree."

In between the two polarities of hot and cold are countless degrees of warmth and coolness. It's the same way with every apparent opposite: hard and soft, noisy and quiet, light and dark, good and bad, love and fear. When you find one thing, you'll also find the potential for its opposite.

The Principle of Polarity empowers you to transmute an undesirable situation to the other end of the pole and manifest a desirable situation. If something undesirable is present in your life, it means that its "opposite" is also present.

This principle works by lifting your mental vibrations to a higher level to banish the undesirable and attract the desirable. Let's use the example of money. One end of the money pole is "prosperity," where you have as much money as you could possibly desire. "Poor" is at the other end, where there isn't enough money to meet your needs. In between these two extremes are countless financial situations in between poverty and prosperity.

Prosperity

Poverty

The Money Pole

If you worry about money or complain that you don't have enough, your thoughts are toward the "Poverty" end of the pole. Consequently, that's what you'll attract. Even if you don't seem to have money right now, you can use the Principle of Polarity to improve your financial situation.

Imagine a lever sliding up and down the Money Pole. To attract more money, you can adjust your vibration upward by visualizing that the lever is at the highest possible location along the pole. Since this pole is in your mind, it's your creation; therefore, it's your personal Money Pole. Even if you're worried about money, you can mentally will the lever to move up higher. That visualization can immediately attract windfalls of prosperity, provided that you monitor the lever's position to ensure that it stays at the upper ends of the pole.

If you have difficulty imagining prosperity, then mentally push the lever on the Money Pole to the highest position that you can imagine manifesting in reality. There's no point in asking you to visualize something that you can't accept as a real possibility. Yet, any improvement in elevating your lever up the Money Pole will have a positive effect on your finances. This is true even if you can only imagine pushing your lever up one notch above its current position. Keep monitoring the Money Pole, and push the lever up as high as you feel comfortable. The minute that you believe that prosperity is possible, you'll allow the lever to reach the top of the pole.

Of course, you can also imagine a pole that controls your beliefs about money and other life areas. Keep your levers high atop these poles to release old, limiting beliefs about money, love, and such.

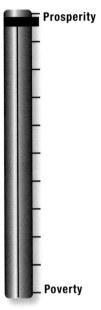

Keep your lever high up the pole.

Everything that you desire has a pole assigned to it, whether it's health, a happy marriage, inner peace, or any other topic. Imagine this whole series of poles with sliding levers, similar to a sound mixing board in a recording studio, or like an airplane's control panel. Each of those levers controls your finances, relationships, health, and other life areas.

Take a moment to visualize your inner control panel. Where are the levers positioned along the poles? To improve any situation, mentally move the lever higher up the pole (and to the top, ideally). Check your poles regularly, or if you ever feel upset, to ensure that they haven't slid downward. This gives a whole new meaning to "staying on top"!

For instance, let's say that you've quarreled with a loved one and you want a peaceful resolution. First, visualize a pole governing your relationship with this person. Mentally move the lever alongside the pole to the top position of "Peaceful Relationship with [name of person]." Every time you think about this person, check to make sure that the lever is still at the top of the pole.

Use this same mental imagery as frequently as possible for other areas of your life. The result is pure Divine magic!

◇◆◇

"Everything is dual; everything has poles; everything has its pair of opposites; like and unlike are the same; opposites are identical in nature, but different in degree; extremes meet; all truths are but half-truths; all paradoxes may be reconciled." — **The Kybalion**

The great fourth Hermetic principle, the Principle of Polarity, embodies the truth that all manifested things have two sides, aspects, or poles. The difference between things seemingly diametrically opposed to each other is only a matter of degree of vibration. For instance, Spirit and Matter are two extremes of the same thing, with intermediate planes in between them. So it is that The All and its creations are upon the same pole, with only vibrational differences between them.

Heat and cold are identical in nature, distinguishable only by degrees. The thermometer shows many degrees of temperature, the lowest being "cold," and the highest "heat." Between these two extremes are many degrees of "hot" or "cold." The higher of two degrees is always "warmer," while the lower is always "colder." There is no absolute standard, as it's a matter of degree. There is no place on the thermometer where heat ceases and cold begins. It is all a matter of higher or lower vibrations. The very terms "high" and "low" are poles of the same thing, and the terms are relative.

It's the same with "east and west." If you travel around the world in an eastward direction, you'll eventually reach a point which is called west at your starting point. Travel far enough north, and you'll find yourself traveling south, or vice versa.

Light and darkness are another example of poles of the same thing, with many degrees between them. In the same way, a musical scale begins with a "C" note. You move upward along the musical scale until you reach another "C," and so on. The differences between the two ends of the scale are the same. Color, too, follows the same principle, with higher and lower vibrations being the only difference between high violet and low red. Large and small are relative. So are noise and quiet, hard and soft, sharp and dull, and positive and negative.

Good and bad are also relative. We call one end of the scale good and the other bad. A thing is "less good" than the thing higher up the scale. However, that "less good" thing, in turn, is "more good" than the thing below it, and so on.

And so it is on the Mental Plane. Love and hate are generally regarded as being diametrically opposed to each other and unreconcilable. But as we apply the Principle of Polarity, we find that there is no such thing as Absolute Love or Absolute Hate, as distinguished from each other. They are merely terms applied to the two poles of the same thing. Beginning at any point of the scale we find "more love," or "less hate," as we ascend, and "more hate" or "less love" as we descend. There are degrees of love and hate and a middle point where like and dislike become indistinguishable. Courage and fear come under the same rule. These pairs of opposites exist everywhere, and wherever you find one thing, you'll find its opposite at the other extreme of the same pole.

This fact enables you to transmute one mental state into another, along the lines of polarization. Things belonging to different classes cannot be transmuted into each other, but things of the same class may have their polarity changed. So, love never becomes east or west, or red or violet. But love may and often does turn into hate. Likewise, hate may be transformed into love, by changing its polarity.

Courage may be transmuted into fear, and the reverse. Hard things may be rendered soft. Dull things become sharp. Hot things become cold. It's all the same process. The transmutation always involves things of the same kind of different degrees. Take the case of a fearful man. By raising his mental vibrations along the line of fear and courage, he can be filled with the highest degree of courage and fearlessness. And, likewise, the slothful person may change himself into an active, energetic individual simply by polarizing along the lines of the desired quality.

The two ends of the poles may be classified as positive and negative. Love is positive to the negative hate, positive courage to negative fear, positive activity to negative non-activity, and so forth. The positive pole is of a higher degree than the negative and readily dominates it. The tendency of nature is in the direction of the dominant activity of the positive pole. So you see that you can change your mental state by moving upward toward the positive pole, and that nature will help you along.

In addition to changing the poles of your own conditions, the Principle of Polarization allows you to also influence another's mind to elevate their mental state. Mental induction means that mental states may be produced by "induction" from others. So a higher mental vibrational rate may be communicated to another person, elevating the polarity of that person's mental state. This is how the majority of "mental treatments" occur.

For instance, let's say that a person is depressed and filled with fear. A mental scientist uses her will to increase the vibration of her own mind. Then she extends this positive vibration to the other person to produce a similarly high vibration through induction. This raises the other person's vibrations and results in polarization at the positive end of the scale. Fear and other negativity are transmuted into courage and similar positive mental states. A little study will show you that these mental changes are all along the line of polarization, with changes only being within a few degrees of another.

This great Hermetic principle enables us to better understand our own mental states, and those of other people. We see that these states are all matters of degree, and that we can raise or lower the vibration at will to change our mental poles. We can master our mental states, instead of being their servant and slave.

And by this knowledge, we can aid others intelligently, and positively raise their polarity. We advise all students to familiarize themselves with this Principle of Polarity, because a correct understanding will throw light on many subjects.

Chapter Ten

SACRED PRINCIPLE
NUMBER FIVE:
THE PRINCIPLE OF
RHYTHM

The Principle of Rhythm ties together the Principles of Correspondence, Vibration, and Polarity. This principle states that everything moves pendulum-like, up and down the poles discussed in the previous chapter.

The cycle of life illustrates these rhythms with birth, life, death, and rebirth. Ocean tides and seasons are other examples. The Hermetists say that the Principle of Rhythm explains changes in moods, feelings, and experiences.

The two ends of our personal Mental Plane poles are Higher and Lower Consciousness (or the higher self and the ego). Until we become aware of the Principles of Polarity and Rhythm, the pendulum swings back and forth between the higher and lower selves. It can feel as if we have no control over our thoughts and their resulting circumstances.

The Hermetists have learned how to neutralize this tendency by making the conscious decision to be unaffected by the pendulum swings of life. *The Kybalion* puts it this way: "The Hermetic Master, or advanced student, polarizes himself at the desired pole and by a process akin to 'refusing' to participate in the backward swing, or, if you prefer, a 'denial' of its influence over him, he stands firm in his polarized position, and allows the mental pendulum to swing back along the unconscious plane."

Visualize the control panel discussed in Chapter 9, and mentally slide all the levers to their highest positions.

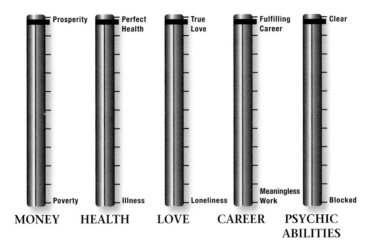

MONEY	HEALTH	LOVE	CAREER	PSYCHIC ABILITIES

To manifest at a consistently high rate, keep your mental poles fixed at the highest points.

This visualization can help you avoid the belief that "bad follows good," or experiencing depression following elation. If you ever become angry, discouraged, or feel bad in any way, remember to check your "control panel." The Principle of Rhythm says that in life, you'll experience changes and fluctuations. But you can be like the wise sailor who stays clear of the swinging boom mast on the ship. You don't have to be affected by life's ups and downs, if you'll just keep your mental control panel levers in their high positions continuously!

Visualize a lock that holds your levers at their highest position, to ensure their consistent elevation.

The Kybalion says: "An understanding of the workings of this Principle will give one the key to the Mastery of these rhythmic swings of feeling. . . ." In other words, the power of your decision can help you ride a continual tide of upward swings.

"Everything flows, out and in; everything has its tides; all things rise and fall; the pendulum-swing manifests in everything; the measure of the swing to the right is the measure of the swing to the left; rhythm compensates" — **The Kybalion**

The great fifth Hermetic principle, the Principle of Rhythm, embodies the truth that everything moves in measured motion. This could also be described as a to-and-from movement, a flow and inflow, a swing forward and backward, a pendulum-like movement, a tide-like ebb and flow, and a high-tide and a low-tide. This steady movement occurs along the poles within the physical, mental, and spiritual planes.

The Principle of Rhythm is closely connected with the Principle of Polarity described in the preceding chapter. Rhythm swings between the two poles established by the Principle of Polarity. This does not mean, however, that the pendulum of Rhythm swings to the extreme poles. This rarely happens. In fact, it's difficult to establish the extreme polar opposites in the majority of cases. But the swing forever goes toward the direction of the pole's extremes even if it never reaches them.

There is always an action and reaction, an advance and retreat, and a rising and sinking manifested in all of the planes of the Universe. Suns, worlds, men, animals, plants, minerals, forces, energy, mind, matter, and even Spirit manifest this principle. Rhythm manifests in the creation and destruction of worlds, in the rise and fall of nations in the life history of all things, and in the mental states of humans.

Universes begin and end with the exhaling and inhaling of The All. Universes are created, reach their extreme point of materiality, and then begin their upward swing toward Spirit. Suns spring into being, achieve their height of power, and the process of retrogression begins. After eons they become dead masses of matter, awaiting another impulse to spark their inner energies into activity to begin a new solar life cycle.

All the worlds are born, grow, and die, only to be reborn. This is how it is with everything swinging from action to reaction and from birth to death. Every being goes through the cycle of birth, growth, maturity, decadence, death, and then new birth. The swing of the pendulum is evident everywhere.

Think of the days and the seasons: night follows day, and day night. The pendulum swings from summer to winter, and back again. The electrons, atoms, molecules, and all masses of matter swing around the circle of their nature. There is no such thing as absolute rest, or cessation from movement.

The Principle of Rhythm has universal application. It may be applied to any question, phenomenon, and all phases of human activity. The Principle of Rhythm is well understood by modern science, and is considered a universal law applicable to material things. The Hermetists carry this principle much further, though. Its manifestations and influence extend to human mental activities. It accounts for the bewildering succession of moods, feelings, and other annoying and perplexing changes that we notice in ourselves. By studying this principle, the Hermetists have learned to escape from troublesome rhythms through the process of Transmutation.

The Law of Neutralization

There were two general planes of consciousness: the lower and the higher. You can rise to the higher plane and escape the swing of the rhythmic pendulum on the lower plane. You do this with the Law of Neutralization, which means having a conscious awareness of the Principle of Rhythm's effect upon your mental states. Without this conscious awareness, you are subject to the pendulum swings of mental states and moods without knowing why.

The Law of Neutralization is akin to rising above a thing and letting it pass beneath you. You polarize yourself at the desired pole, and then refuse to participate in the backward swing. This helps you to stay stable and be unaffected as the mental pendulum swings back along the unconscious plane.

All individuals who have attained any degree of self-mastery accomplish this, more or less unknowingly. By refusing to allow their moods and negative mental states to affect them, they apply the Law of Neutralization. The master, however, carries this to a much higher degree of proficiency. Through the use of will, the master attains a steady degree of poise and mental centeredness, without being swung backward and forward by the mental pendulum of moods and feelings. You, too, can attain this through practice and commitment.

If you've been a creature of moods, feelings, and emotion in the past, you can alter this course and have mastery of yourself. Consider how much these swings of rhythm have affected your life and how your enthusiasm has been invariably followed by feelings of depression. Likewise, your periods of courage were likely succeeded by equal moods of fear.

Perhaps you never suspected that your feelings rose and fell like tides according to natural law. An understanding of the workings of this Principle can give you mastery over these rhythmic swings of feeling. This enables you to know yourself better, and avoid being carried away by inflows and outflows. The will is superior to the conscious manifestation of this Principle, although the Principle itself can never be destroyed. You may escape its effects, but the Principle operates nevertheless. The pendulum ever swings, although you may avoid being carried along with it.

The Law of Compensation

The Principle of Rhythm also incorporates the Law of Compensation. One of the definitions of the word "compensate" is "to counterbalance," which is how Hermetists use the term. When The Kybalion says "the measure of the swing to the right is the measure of the swing to the left; rhythm compensates," it is referring to the Law of Compensation.

The Law of Compensation holds that the swing in one direction determines the swing in the opposite direction. One swing balances, and the other counterbalances. We see many examples of this law on the physical plane. For instance, the pendulum of the clock swings a certain distance to the right, and then an equal distance to the left. The seasons balance each other in the same way. Ocean tides do the same.

When the pendulum swings a short distance in one direction, its backward swing is equally short. Long swings to and fro are also equivalent to one another. The Law of Compensation applies to both the material and mental planes. So a person who experiences great suffering has more capability of feeling great joy, because of the extreme swings. In contrast, a person with blunted emotions won't feel extreme pain or joy. The capacity for pain and pleasure is balanced within each individual.

Hermetists teach that before we can enjoy great pleasure, we must have swung as far proportionately toward the other pole of feeling. This does not mean that "bad follows good," however. In fact, the opposite is true as the negative proceeds the positive. Pleasure is the rhythmic swing that compensates for pain previously experienced in this life or past lives. This throws a new light on the problem of pain.

◇◇◇◇

It is entirely possible, as many have done, to escape the rhythmic swing toward pain, by the process of Neutralization previously described. By consciously rising to the higher mental plane, much of the experience that comes from the lower plane is avoided and escaped. This will require commitment and practice on your part, but the results are well worth any effort involved.

Chapter Eleven

SACRED PRINCIPLE
NUMBER SIX:
THE PRINCIPLE OF
CAUSE AND EFFECT

The Principle of Cause and Effect states that nothing happens by chance. Everything in the Universe has an identifiable cause. When something appears to occur by chance, it means that the cause is unrecognized.

Causes aren't creators of events or circumstances. They're catalysts in a long chain of them, usually driven by underlying beliefs about life and "the way that it is." For instance, if you believe that you won't be hired for your dream job, you'll never apply for it. Yet, this belief is only one factor in a chain of causes. For instance, where did the belief come from? If you say, "Well my parents modeled it for me," then there's still the question of where your parents acquired this belief, so there's no point in tracing through chains of events in search of a primary cause. The important and more helpful point is to develop an awareness of this principle in your own life.

Without an awareness of cause and effect, you may be unduly influenced by external factors, such as the desires of those exerting willful force in your direction. Hermetics says that you can't change or stop the principles and laws. You can, however, use higher will to prevail against lower will.

A conscious awareness of cause and effect, combined with intention and practice, helps you rise above external influences. *The Kybalion* says that this conscious awareness helps us to become "movers in the game of life instead of pawns, Causes instead of Effects."

Notice any strong thoughts or feelings that you have throughout the day. These can be thoughts and feelings that seem to just "pop in" of their own accord, or ones that are consciously manifested. Be aware of recurring thoughts and feelings, especially those involving strong feelings.

As you notice these intense thoughts and feelings, immediately visualize your mental control panel. Observe whether the pole levers have slid downward, or whether they remain upward, in response to your strong feelings and thoughts. Use your will to lift any levers that have slid down. The action of keeping your levers high is a cause that yields desirable effects. It is the key to Divine magic!

*"Every Cause has its Effect; every Effect has its Cause;
everything happens according to Law; Chance is but a
name for Law not recognized; there are many planes of
causation, but nothing escapes the Law." — **The Kybalion**

The great sixth Hermetic principle is the Principle of Cause and
Effect, which embodies the truth that Law pervades the Universe.
Nothing happens by chance. In fact, "chance" indicates that an
unrecognized cause exists.

The Principle of Cause and Effect underlies all scientific thought,
and was enunciated by Hermetic teachers in the earliest days. Philosophers throughout the ages have all agreed about this principle,
arguing only about the details of its operation. The underlying Principle of Cause and Effect has been accepted by practically all the
influential thinkers of the world.

A little consideration will show that there's no such thing as
chance. Webster's defines the word "chance" as: "Something that
happens unpredictably without discernible human intention or ob-
servable cause; the assumed impersonal purposeless determiner of
unaccountable happenings."

Yet, how could an agent such as "chance" exist independent of
the universal laws, order, and continuity? Such an agent would be*

entirely independent of the orderly Universe, and therefore superior to it. Nothing outside of The All could be outside of Universal Law, because The All is Law itself. There is no room in the Universe for something outside of and independent of Law. The existence of such a thing would render all natural laws ineffective, and would plunge the Universe into chaotic disorder and lawlessness.

"Chance" is an expression relating to obscure causes that we cannot perceive or understand. The term is often used to describe the rolling of dice. Yet, each time a die falls and displays a certain number, it obeys a law as infallible as that which governs the revolution of the planets around the sun. The chain of causes that result in the die falling with certain numbers showing include the initial position of the die, the amount of muscular energy expended in the throw, the condition of the table, and so forth. Behind these visible causes are chains of unseen preceding causes which influence the number showing on the die.

If a die is cast many times, the numbers shown will be about equal. Toss a penny in the air a sufficient number of times, and heads and tails will show equally as it falls. This is the operation of the law of average. But both the average and the single toss come under the Principle of Cause and Effect. The causes preceding the throw of the dice make it impossible for the die to fall in any other way than it does each time. Given the same causes, the same results will follow. There is always a "cause" and a "because" to every event. Nothing ever happens without a cause, or rather a chain of causes.

No event creates another event, but is merely a link in the great orderly chain of events flowing from the creative energy of The All. There is a continuity between everything that has gone before, and everything that follows. A stone is dislodged from a mountain side and crashes through the roof of a cottage in the valley below. At first sight we regard this as a chance effect, but when we examine the matter we find a great chain of causes behind it. There was the rain that softened the earth supporting the stone and allowed it to fall. Before that was the influence of the sun, wind, and other rains, which gradually disintegrated the piece of rock from a larger piece. Prior to that were the causes that led to the formation of the mountain, and its upheaval by convulsions of nature, and so on. Still other causes include the factors behind the rain and the roof. Each event has a boggling series of causes and effects.

Similarly, each person has two birth parents, four grandparents, eight great-grandparents, sixteen great-great-grandparents, and so on. If a certain man had not met a certain lady, way back in the dim periods of human history, you may not be here now. If the same couple hadn't met, perhaps we who write this book would also not be here. Yourself, this book, and its authors also live in a chain of events that are affecting the future. The ancestry of causes behind even the most trifling event shows the relativity and association of all things. Every thought we think and every act we perform has its direct and indirect results within the great chain of Cause and Effect. Nothing is large or small in the Mind of The All, because they're all connected.

This discussion may also trigger questions about free will or Determinism. According to Hermetic teachings, neither side of the free will controversy is entirely correct. In fact, both sides are partially right. The Principle of Polarity shows that both are half-truths on opposing ends of the pole of Truth. Humans are both free and yet bound by necessity.

Some people are slaves to their heredity and environment, and enjoy very little freedom. They are swayed by the opinions, customs, and thoughts of the outside world, and also by their emotions, feelings, and moods. They claim that they are free to do whatever they want to, without analyzing the reasons why they want to do something.

Too many people are carried along like the falling stone, obedient to environment, outside influences, internal moods, and the desires and wills of others stronger than themselves. Moved like the pawns on the checkerboard of life, they play their parts and are laid aside after the game is over.

But those who have learned self-mastery understand the rules of the game. They rise above the plane of material life, and place themselves in touch with the higher powers of their nature. They determine their own moods, energy levels, and polarities, as well as the environment surrounding them. They become movers in the game, instead of pawns—Causes instead of Effects.

These masters don't escape the causation of the higher planes. They simply work with the higher laws, and so master circumstances on the lower plane. They form a conscious part of the Law, instead of being its blind instruments. While they serve on the higher planes, they rule on the material plane.

On the higher and lower planes, the Law is always in operation. There is no such thing as chance, and everything is governed by Universal Law. The infinite number of laws are manifestations of the One Great Law: The Law which is The All.

No sparrow drops unnoticed by the Mind of The All. Even the hairs on our head are numbered. There is nothing outside of Law, and nothing that happens contrary to it. And yet, we are not blind slaves to these laws. The Hermetic teachings are that humans may use Law to overcome laws. The higher will always prevails against the lower.

Chapter Twelve

SACRED PRINCIPLE NUMBER SEVEN: THE PRINCIPLE OF GENDER

When the Hermetists use the term *gender,* they're referring to masculine and feminine energies that combine to create manifestations. Gender has nothing to do with physical sexual attributes.

Every person, thing, and situation has both masculine and feminine energies. A woman has inner male and female energy. Likewise with a man. It's the same male-female balance throughout life, from the tiniest atoms up to the largest mountains. Atoms have masculine and feminine energies that bond to create matter. In fact, feminine and masculine energies are always combining and catalyzing each other with resulting creations.

Masculine energy sends itself outward into the world. Feminine energy is receptive and attracting. Outwardly projecting masculine energies are called *positive,* and receptive feminine energies are called *negative.* The terms *positive* and *negative* aren't used in the usual sense of good and bad. They refer only to the direction in which energy flows, like the plus and minus signs on a battery.

The Principle of Gender works on all three planes of correspondence: physical, mental, and spiritual. On the mental plane, masculine energy is expressed as the conscious mind, and feminine energy is the unconscious mind.

Mental Gender

Hermetists distinguish between the "Me" and the "I" within each person. Your Me is a combination of your moods, mental states, habits, and body. It's your feminine energy. Your I is the being within you who can will the Me to act according to its wishes, desires, and intentions. It's your masculine energy.

Many identify only with their Me state. They feel victimized and constricted by the Me's vacillating moods. The Me isn't undesirable, though. In fact, it has creative energy force within it. However, the Me needs to be balanced with the I, the male and the female together, to use the creative force in consistent ways.

The Feminine Mental Principle (Me energy) is receptive, and generates new ideas that your Masculine Mental Principle (I energy) puts into action. If you can detach from identifying with your Me and instead identify with your I, you can then send energy and direction to the Me. Your Me and I will then team up to manifest the Me's wonderful ideas into reality.

The I is the force that makes sure that all the levers on the console are kept consistently high. Even when they slip down, the I can observe and correct this.

Telepathy and other psychic phenomena can also be explained and improved through the Principle of Gender. Telepathy occurs when a thought is sent (which is a masculine action) by one person and then received (a feminine action) by another person. Telepathy can further be developed through practicing receptiveness, such as asking others to help you and saying yes to gifts and offers of assistance.

Often, people who are psychically blocked and unable to see or feel angels or other psychic energies are those who are such generous givers that they rarely allow themselves to receive. This makes them unbalanced in their male energy, and so it's difficult for them to relax and become aware of the inflow of Spirit. People who have competitive or high-stress jobs often get overly situated in their male energy.

Another psychic block occurs when a person tries too hard to make a psychic vision happen. Striving is a male energy. Receptiveness is the feminine energy required to receive psychic impressions. So, too much male energy can block you from receiving spiritual messages.

An imbalance of too much feminine energy is equally unhealthy, often resulting in a passive personality who merely observes life rather than acting upon or expressing original thoughts and ideas. Balanced energy is the healthiest, both for psychic development and also for practicing Divine magic.

"Gender is in everything; everything has its Masculine and Feminine Principles; Gender manifests on all planes."
— ***The Kybalion***

The great seventh Hermetic principle, the Principle of Gender, embodies the truth that gender is manifested in everything. The Masculine and Feminine principles are ever-present and active in all phases of phenomena and on each plane of life. Gender, in its Hermetic sense, and "sex" in the ordinarily accepted use of the term, are not the same.

The word "gender" is derived from the Latin root meaning "to beget, procreate, generate, create, or produce." This word has a much broader meaning than the term "sex," which refers to the physical distinctions between male and female beings. Sex is merely a manifestation of gender on the Great Physical Plane.

In contrast, the effects of gender's creating, producing, and generating are visible on every plane. For instance, we find manifestations of the Principle of Gender among the protons, ions, and electrons, which constitute the basis of matter. These protons, electrons, and ions revolve around each other and vibrate at a high degree and intensity.

But the formation of the atom is really due to the clustering of negative electrons around a positive one. The protons influence the electrons, causing the latter to assume certain combinations and so "create" or "generate" an atom. This is in line with the most ancient Hermetic teachings, which have always identified the Masculine Principle of Gender with the "positive," and the feminine with the "negative'" poles of electricity.

We aren't using the terms "positive" or "negative" in the ordinary sense where "positive" means something real and strong, and "negative" means weakness. Nothing is further from the real facts of electrical phenomenon. The negative pole of the battery is really the pole through which the production of new forms and energies is manifested. There is nothing "negative" about it.

Science now uses the word "cathode" in place of "negative." The word "cathode" derives from the Greek root meaning "descent, the path of generation." The cathode, or negative pole, is the mother principle of electrical phenomena. Instead of using the terms "cathode" or "negative," though, we shall use the word "feminine" in speaking of that pole of activity.

The attraction of feminine electrons and masculine protons creates atoms. When the feminine electron unites with a masculine proton, the creative process begins. Feminine particles vibrate rapidly under the influence of the masculine energy, and circle rapidly around the latter. The result is the birth of a new atom, composed of a union of the masculine protons and feminine electrons. However when the union is formed, the atom is a separate thing having certain properties. Electrons and protons are the most active workers in nature's field. Their unions create light, heat, electricity, magnetism, attraction, repulsion, chemical affinity, and similar phenomena. All this arises from the Principle of Gender on the plane of energy.

The masculine principle seems to direct energy toward the feminine principle, which starts the creative process. The feminine principle always does the creative work on all planes. Everything in the organic world manifests both genders: The masculine is always present in the feminine form, and the feminine present in the masculine form.

Gender is in constant operation and manifestation in the field of inorganic matter and energy. The scope of this book doesn't allow for a thorough scientific discussion of the phenomena of attraction and repulsion of atoms, chemical affinity, or the attraction or cohesion between the molecules of matter and atomic particles. These facts are too well known to need extended comment from us. Hermetics teaches that all of these activities and phenomena are manifestations of the Gender Principle.

Moreover, the Law of Gravitation (that strange attraction in which all particles and bodies of matter in the Universe tend toward each other) is another manifestation of the Principle of Gender and the attracting the masculine to the feminine energies.

The Principle of Gender and the Mental Plane

Let us now consider the operation of the principle on the mental plane, where many interesting features await examination.

Psychologists speak about the dual-mind, which they label as the "conscious" and the "unconscious." These seemingly new theories have been discussed in Hermetics since ancient times. Dual-mind theories also correspond to the Principle of Gender. The Masculine Principle of Mind corresponds to the conscious mind and the Feminine Principle of Mind corresponds to the unconscious mind.

To get a deeper sense of this teaching, turn your attention in-

ward upon the Self dwelling within you. Your consciousness reports the existence of this Self to you with "I Am" feelings, thoughts, and phrases. Focus a little while longer and you'll realize this "I Am" can be separated into two distinct parts. While these two parts work in unison, they may nevertheless be separated in consciousness.

While at first there seems to be only an "I" existing, a more careful examination reveals that there is both an "I" and a "Me." These mental twins differ in their characteristics, and an examination of this phenomenon will illuminate many of the problems of mental influence.

Let us begin with a consideration of the Me, which is usually mistaken for the I, until you press the inquiry further into the recesses of consciousness. Your Me consists of your feelings, knowledge, tastes, likes, dislikes, habits, and characteristics, which make up your personality. This is the "Self" known to yourself and others. The Me's emotions and feelings change and are subject to the Principles of Rhythm and Polarity, which manifests one extreme of feeling to another.

Some mistakenly believe that their "Me" consists solely of their body and physical appetites. Yet, those who rise in consciousness are able to disentangle their "Me" from the idea of the body. They are able to correctly identify the body as "belonging to" the mental part of themselves. There is still an even higher level through which to view the "Me." Instead of identifying with your feelings and personality, you can see them as aspects within yourself, but which are not truly "You."

Since your mind created these feelings and other states, you can change them with your will. After learning to elevate your moods and outlook at will, you stop identifying with your mental states, emotions, feelings, habits, qualities, characteristics, and other personal mental belongings. You set them aside in the "not me" collection of curiosities and encumbrances. Clearly, this requires much mental concentration and power of mental analysis. Still the task is possible for the advanced student, and even those not so far advanced are able to see, in the imagination, how the process may be performed.

After this detachment process has been performed, you'll find yourself in conscious possession of a "Self" which has "I" and "Me" dual aspects: The "Me" is a mental womb that produces thoughts, ideas, emotions, feelings, and other mental states. The Me reports to the consciousness with creative ideas and inspirations of all sorts and kinds. Its powers of creative energy are enormous. Yet the Me must receive energy from its "I" companion (or another person's I) to manifest its mental creations.

There's an aspect of you that can will your Me to act in certain ways. This same aspect also stands aside and witnesses your mental creations. This aspect is called your "I." It is that part of you in which you can rest your mind, as the I isn't involved in constantly creating ideas like the Me. The I helps the Me put her ideas into motion, by sending her supportive energy. The I wills the Me's ideas into manifestation.

The I represents the Masculine Principle of Mental Gender, and the Me represents the Female Principle. The I is the human aspect of Being, while the Me is the aspect of Becoming. Your Masculine and Feminine Mental Principles co-creations are the same process used when the Mind of The All creates Universes. The two illustrations are similar in kind, although vastly different in degree according to the Principle of Correspondence: "As above, so below; as below, so above."

The Masculine and Feminine Principles—the "I" and the "Me"—are the master-key to understanding mental and psychic phenomena.

The Feminine Principle always tends in the direction of receiving impressions, while the tendency of the Masculine Principle is always in the direction of giving or expressing. The Feminine Principle has a more varied field of operation than the Masculine Principle. The Feminine Principle conducts the work of generating new thoughts, concepts, and ideas, including the work of the imagination. The Masculine Principle contents itself with the work of the "will" in its varied phases. And yet, without the active aid of the Masculine Principle, the Feminine Principle may be passively contented with externally generated mental images, instead of producing original internally generated mental creations.

Those who focus continued attention and thought on a subject are actively employing both of the Mental Principles. They're using the Feminine for mental generation, and the Masculine Will in stimulating and energizing the creative portion of the mind. Many people ignore their Masculine Principle. They are content to live according to the thoughts and ideas instilled into the "Me" from the "I" of other minds.

The Principle of Gender is also a key to understanding the various psychic phenomena classified as telepathy and hypnotism. Telepathy occurs when the vibratory energy of the Masculine Principle is projected toward the Feminine Principle of another person and the latter accepts and processes the projected energy. Hypnotism operates in the same way. The Masculine Principle of the hypnotist directs a stream of vibratory energy or will-power toward the Feminine Principle of the other person. The latter accepts this energy and acts and thinks differently as a result. An idea lodged in the mind of another person grows and develops, and is eventually regarded as the rightful offspring of the second person.

It takes practice and strength to use your Masculine willpower consistently. Yet, this effort is worthwhile, because it will direct the otherwise passive Feminine creativity into action. Once you begin working regularly with your own Masculine willpower, you will be less susceptible and in need of other people's Masculine willpower. In other words, you will find your independence of thought, finances, and freedom *through enacting the Principle of Gender within yourself.*

The strong men and women of the world manifest the Masculine Principle of Will, and their strength depends materially upon this fact. Instead of living upon the impressions made upon their minds by others, they dominate their own minds by their will. They obtain desirable mental images and have the option of influencing the minds of others. Strong people implant their seed-thoughts into the minds of the masses of people, causing them to think thoughts in accordance with the desires and wills of the strong individuals. Too many people are sheeplike creatures, never originating an idea of their own, nor using their own powers of mental activity. If they would generate their Masculine Principle, they could escape the herd and be their own shepherds.

The manifestation of Mental Gender may be noticed all around us in everyday life. Magnetic personalities are those who use the Masculine Principle to impress their ideas upon others. The actor who makes people weep or cry as he wills is employing this principle, and so is the successful orator, statesman, preacher, writer, or others in the public spotlight. The peculiar influence exerted by some people over others is due to the manifestation of Mental Gender along the vibrational lines we have described. This principle is the secret of personal magnetism and influence, as well as the phenomena called hypnotism.

The energizing of the Feminine Principle by the vibratory energy of the Masculine Principle is in accordance with the universal laws of nature. The very creation of the Universe follows the same Principle of Gender, along with all creative manifestations upon the spiritual, mental, and physical planes: "As above, so below; as below, so above."

When the principle of Mental Gender is once grasped and understood, the varied psychological and psychic phenomena are understandable. The principle works in practice, because it's based upon the universal laws of life. With the aid of The Kybalion, you may approach any occult library anew. These principles from ancient Egypt illuminate many topics previously considered mysterious. That is the purpose of this book.

We do not come expounding a new philosophy, but rather furnishing the outlines of great old-world teachings which will clarify the teachings of others. May these teaching serve as a Great Reconciler of differing theories, and opposing doctrines. Ultimately, they are all the same, as the Principle of Polarity has reminded us.

HERMETIC AXIOMS

*T*he *Kybalion* offers both philosophical and practical insights that can assist you with any endeavor. The seven principles help to chart the territories of emotions, health, and materiality. The more you study these principles, the more you'll see examples of them in everyday situations. That's when Hermetics begin to make sense, and become incorporated into your life. As lofty as *The Kybalion*'s discussions sound, they really are very down-to-earth.

Hermetics shares the good news that your life can be filled with all things that are desirable, your moods and energy levels can be consistently elevated, and you have all of the means to live a creative and prosperous life.

Since everything in your life is a product of your mind, you can use the tools of Hermetics to make any desired alterations. For instance:

- Anytime you experience an upsetting situation, remember that if the negative is present, so must the positive (or desirable outcome) also be present.

- Mentally check your mental control panel on the pole governing the situation. Push the levers all the way to the top (or as high up as your beliefs will allow). This is a visual representation of the Hermetic Law of Neutralization, which says you can use your will to decide against being pulled downward in your moods, energy, or situations. When your thoughts are elevated, you attract and manifest more desirable outcomes.

- Keep monitoring the pole to ensure that the levers on every area of your life stay high. This will help you to transmute undesirable situations into desirable situations, without strain.

And what about the angels, archangels, goddesses, ascended masters, and other spiritual helpers? As *The Kybalion,* my own books, and many people's experiences attest, these celestial spirits are very involved in our lives. They live on the third plane of Spirit, but they interact with both the physical and the mental planes.

Because they vibrate at a higher frequency than matter or mind, the angelic and ascended master realms can help to elevate us. Just by thinking about angels and divinities, your thoughts are raised to a higher frequency. You can also ask these beings to assist you in keeping the levers high on your mental control panel.

In addition, the Hermetic Principle of Gender can help you generate new ideas and then put them into action. This principle can help you overcome self-doubt or procrastination tendencies.

Your inner feminine energy is receptive and eternally patient, which is why she sometimes appears passive and unmotivated. Like a satellite dish receiver, she's also tapped in to the collective unconscious, which is the generator of wonderful new ideas, innovations, and inspirations. So your inner female is similar to a sensitive and creative artist who has wonderful ideas, but doesn't act upon them.

Your inner masculine energy loves taking action. His energy is giving and enthusiastic, which is why he sometimes feels pushy or domineering. He's all action without the inspiration. Living in either energy too much creates an unhealthy imbalance.

Yet, imagine if your inner sensitive female artist—with all of her wonderful ideas—would work as a teammate with the inner male. It'd be like the artist and the manager/talent agent/producer working together as an unstoppably successful team!

Your feminine energy receives Divinely inspired ideas, which the masculine energy then acts upon. Your inner male breathes life or Spirit into the body of the female's ideas. The rhythm of the masculine and feminine is natural, unless it's blocked by fear, or negative experiences or judgements about one gender.

One way to experience consistently balanced masculine and female energies is to engage in giving and receiving daily. Each day, give something (time, money, friendly words, and so on) without any attachment to receiving praise, rewards, or gratitude from the recipients. This will engage your masculine energy in a healthy way. Also make it a daily habit to receive, to keep your feminine energy alive and awakened. Be a gracious receiver who says "Thank you" without apology or guilt to gifts that are offered.

Your inner female is quietly receptive to the whispers of Divinely inspired ideas. Her teammate, the inner male, is poised to lovingly put these ideas into action. This is the inner mystical marriage that sages have always discussed. This is the spark of Divine magic.

You are both high-priest and high-priestess, wizard and

sorceress. You have the power, right now, to effect great miracles in your life and in those around you. You are forever a Divine magician, and with the help of the seven Hermetic principles, may you forever enjoy the fruits of these gifts!

*"The possession of Knowledge, unless accompanied by a manifestation and expression in action, is like the hoarding of precious metals: a vain and foolish thing. Knowledge, like wealth, is intended for use. The Law of Use is Universal, and he who violates it suffers by reason of his conflict with natural forces." — **The Kybalion***

The above quotation, stated forcibly by The Kybalion, refers to The Law of Use. This Law says that knowledge without use and expression is a vain thing which brings no good to its possessor, or to the human race. Beware of mental miserliness, in which you hoard your ideas and inspirations. Instead, express into action that which you have learned. Study the axioms within <u>The Kybalion</u>, but practice them, also.

Hermetic teachings were kept securely locked in the minds of its teachers and students during times of religious intolerance. Yet, Hermes intended for these principles to be taught, studied, and put into practice.

We give below some of the more important Hermetic Axioms from The Kybalion, with a few comments added to each. Make these your own, and practice and use them, for they are not really your own until you have used them.

"To change your mood or mental state, change your vibration."
*— **The Kybalion***

You may change your mental vibrations by directing your will and attention in the direction of a more desirable state. Will directs the attention, and attention changes the vibration. Cultivate the Art of Attention, by means of the will, and you hold the secret to the mastery of moods and mental states.

*"To destroy an undesirable rate of mental vibration, put into operation the Principle of Polarity and concentrate upon the opposite pole to that which you desire to suppress. Kill out the undesirable by changing its polarity." — **The Kybalion***

This is one of the most important of the Hermetic formulas. It is based upon true scientific principles. We have shown you that a mental state and its opposite were merely the two poles of one thing, and that by Mental Transmutation the polarity might be reversed. This principle is known to psychologists, who apply it to the breaking up of undesirable habits by bidding their students concentrate upon the opposite quality.

If you are fearful, don't waste time trying to "kill out" fear. Instead, cultivate the quality of courage, and fear will disappear. This is similar to turning on a light to illuminate a dark room, instead of fighting the darkness.

To banish a negative quality, concentrate upon the Positive Pole of that same quality, and the vibrations will gradually change from Negative to Positive, until finally you will become polarized on the Positive Pole instead of the Negative. The reverse is also true, as many have found out to their sorrow, when they have allowed themselves to vibrate too constantly on the Negative pole of things.

By changing your polarity you may master your moods, change your mental states, remake your disposition, and build up character. Much of the mental mastery of Hermetics comes from this application of polarity, which is one of the important aspects of mental transmutation. Remember this axiom from The Kybalion: *"Mind (as well as metals and elements) may be transmuted from state to state, degree to degree, condition to condition, pole to pole, vibration to vibration."*

The mastery of polarization is the mastery of the mental transmutation or mental alchemy. Unless you acquire the art of changing your own polarity, you will be unable to affect your environment. An understanding of this principle will enable you to change your polarity, as well as that of others, if you will devote the time, care, study, and practice necessary to master the art. The principle is true, but the results obtained depend upon your persistent patience and practice.

> *"Rhythm may be neutralized by an application of the Art of Polarization." — **The Kybalion***

As we have explained in previous chapters, the Principle of Rhythm manifests on the mental and physical planes. The bewildering succession of moods, feelings, emotions, and other mental states are due to the backward and forward swing of the mental pendulum, which carries us from one extreme of feeling to the other.

The Law of Neutralization enables you to overcome the operation of rhythm in consciousness. As we have explained, there are higher and lower planes of consciousness. By rising mentally and dwelling on your higher plane of consciousness, you escape the backward swing to lower consciousness. Through an act of will, you polarize on the Higher Self, which raises your mental vibrations above the lower plane of consciousness. You rise above the pendulum swing and allow it to pass beneath you.

You can polarize yourself at the positive pole of your being, the "I Am" pole, rather than the pole of personality. You can refuse and deny the operation of Rhythm. This decision raises you above the *lower plane of consciousness. Stand firm in your Statement of Being as you allow the pendulum to swing back to the lower plane without affecting you. This is accomplished by all individuals who have attained any degree of self-mastery, whether they understand the law or not. Such persons simply refuse to be swung by the pendulum of mood and emotion, and they remain polarized on the positive pole.*

This process doesn't involve destroying the Principle of Rhythm, since that's impossible. You simply overcome one law by counterbalancing it with another to maintain emotional equilibrium. The laws of balance and counterbalance operate on the mental and physical planes. Once you understand and work with these principles, you will seem to overthrow natural laws. However, what you're really doing is practicing counterbalance. You are rising to a higher plane of causation, which counterbalances the laws of the lower planes of causation.

*"Nothing escapes the Principle of Cause and Effect, but there are many Planes of Causation, and one may use the laws of the higher to overcome the laws of the lower." — **The Kybalion***

By rising above the plane of ordinary causes, you become a Cause instead of being merely Caused. When you master your moods and feelings, and therefore neutralize Rhythm, you escape Cause and Effect on the ordinary plane. Too many people are carried along, obedient to their environment, the stronger wills of others, the effects of inherited tendencies, and other outward causes that move them on the chessboard of life like pawns.

By rising above these influencing causes, you enjoy a higher plane of mental action. By dominating your moods, emotions, impulses, and feelings, you express new qualities and powers that help you to overcome your ordinary environment and become players instead of pawns. You then play the game of life intelligently, instead of being manipulated by external influences, powers, wills. You use the Principle of Cause and Effect, instead of being used by it.

Of course, even avatars are subject to this Principle's manifestations on the higher planes. But on the lower planes of activity, they are masters instead of slaves. As <u>The Kybalion</u> says: "The wise ones serve on the higher, but rule on the lower. They obey the laws coming from above them. But on their own plane and those below them, they rule and give orders. And, yet, in so doing, they form a part of the Principle, instead of opposing it.

"The wise person falls in with the Law, and by understanding its movements, operates it instead of being its blind slave. The skilled swimmer turns this way and that way, going and coming at will, instead of being as the log which is carried here and there. Yet both swimmer and log, wise person and fool, are subject to Law. 'He who understands this is well on the road to Mastery.'" — ***The Kybalion***

In conclusion, let's review again the Hermetic Axiom:

"True Hermetic Transmutation is a Mental Art."
— The Kybalion

The process of influencing your environment is accomplished by mental power. Since the Universe is wholly mental, it's logical that it may be ruled only by mentality.

This truth explains all the phenomena and manifestations of the various mental powers that are taught and studied. Within every phenomenon and teaching is the ever-present Principle of the Mental Substance of the Universe. If the Universe is Mental, then it follows that Mental Transmutation must change the conditions and phenomena of the Universe. If the Universe is Mental, then Mind must be the highest power affecting its phenomena. If this is understood, then you will understand and work "miracles."

Remember: "The All is Mind; The Universe is Mental."
— The Kybalion

ABOUT THE AUTHOR

Doreen Virtue, Ph.D., is a fourth-generation metaphysician who holds B.A., M.A., and Ph.D. degrees in psychology. She's a longtime student of philosophical studies, and minored in philosophy in college. Doreen has taught about Hermes and Hermetic teachings in her international workshops and in her books *Angel Medicine* and *Goddesses & Angels*.

She has appeared on *Oprah*, CNN, *Good Morning America*, *Richard & Judy* (UK), *Kerri-Anne* (Australia), and other media worldwide.

For information on her workshops, books, or other products, please visit her Website at: **www.AngelTherapy.com**.

We hope you enjoyed this Hay House book. If you'd like to receive a free catalog featuring additional Hay House books and products, or if you'd like information about the Hay Foundation, please contact:

Hay House, Inc.
P.O. Box 5100
Carlsbad, CA 92018-5100

(760) 431-7695 or (800) 654-5126
(760) 431-6948 (fax) or (800) 650-5115 (fax)
www.hayhouse.com® • www.hayfoundation.org

***

Published and distributed in Australia by: Hay House Australia Pty. Ltd.
18/36 Ralph St. • Alexandria NSW 2015 • *Phone:* 612-9669-4299
Fax: 612-9669-4144 • www.hayhouse.com.au

Published and distributed in the United Kingdom by: Hay House UK, Ltd.
292B Kensal Rd., London W10 5BE • *Phone:* 44-20-8962-1230
Fax: 44-20-8962-1239 • www.hayhouse.co.uk

Published and distributed in the Republic of South Africa by:
Hay House SA (Pty), Ltd., P.O. Box 990, Witkoppen 2068
Phone/Fax: 27-11-706-6612 • orders@psdprom.co.za

Published in India by:
Hay House Publications (India) Pvt. Ltd., Muskaan Complex,
Plot No. 3, B-2, Vasant Kunj, New Delhi 110 070
Phone: 91-11-4176-1620 • *Fax:* 91-11-4176-1630 • www.hayhouseindia.co.in

Distributed in Canada by: Raincoast • 9050 Shaughnessy St., Vancouver, B.C.
V6P 6E5 • *Phone:* (604) 323-7100 • *Fax:* (604) 323-2600 • www.raincoast.com